A Language Yardstick

Understanding and Assessment

Priscilla L. Vail

MODERN LEARNING PRESS
ROSEMONT, NJ

ISBN 1–56762–084–1

A Language Yardstick:
Understanding and Assessment

Item #616

To
those who help me
try to measure up

Thanks to my colleagues, students, friends, children, children-in-law, and grandchildren, who offer me the inches, feet, and yards of language in all its glorious combinations.

Thanks to Robert Low, my editor, for the friendship and mutual professional respect hammered out of discourse, persuasion, and resolution.

CONTENTS

INTRODUCTION

When I was a child, my parents glued two yardsticks to the inner side of the linen-closet door jamb. The lower one, starting at floor level, measured the inches from 1 to 36. The higher yardstick was turned over, showing the numbers from 37 to 72. Then, because the door frame was 7 feet high, my father hand lettered the remaining numbers and intervals from 73 to 84. The outer edge of the jamb was for recording the heights, growths, and upward stretchings of family, close friends, or lone visitors at Thanksgiving.

Now, my husband and I have taken on the tradition. We measure with ceremony! The child stands, ramrod straight, against the edge of the jamb. The adult levels a book on the head of the measuree, who then steps away. The recorder, holding the volume steady, makes an indelible mark for height, adding the initials of the measuree and the date. Recorded for posterity are yardstick histories of who reached what heights and when.

In a funny example, when one aunt and uncle brought their infant, they held the baby up against the jamb, the book ceremony was carried out, and the baby's initials and date (JML 11/24/42) remain to this day. He and, now, his progeny take great delight in reviewing his progress, starting at 25" tall, moving up to the level of the lock, and then stretching well beyond to his adult height of 6'4".

Each person has marks signifying level and demonstrating growth. For example, Daphne was 3" above the knob for a while, and her brother, Stephen (younger by two years), an inch below it. Three years later they were even, and today Stephen has soared. Daphne has leveled off. Some are moving upward and passing her, others cluster at higher or lower levels.

The door jamb isn't a contest. The point is that *everyone* is *somewhere* on the progression.

The same thing is true of language development. *Everyone* is *somewhere* on the continuum. All people start at the lower end and move upward as they wobble, aim, or grasp for higher levels. Usually, children of roughly the same age will reach similar levels, even though we expect variation in language development, just as we expect variations in physical height and weight. A group of 4-year-olds usually have clustering though not identical results (scores, patterns) in physical dimensions; not all are the same, yet many are normal. Similarly, pre-adolescents scatter across grids of intellectual achievement, basketball prowess, or language skill.

In this book, we will focus on language development in the years between pre-school and fourth grade, and even beyond. Laboratory researchers compile statistics and norms, educators recognize the importance of language in school, parents bewail their kids' slang. But without a reliable language yardstick handy, most people have trouble measuring what is normal, average, or sub-standard. This small book is designed to change that by providing information on how language develops, indicating how to know when kids are on target, and offering practical suggestions for those who aren't. The suggestions, by and large, are either free or very inexpensive; many are variations on old favorites and parlor games.

This is *not* a book about decoding skills, per se, or how to teach reading. This is *not* a manual on how to get a child into a 3.5 reader by Thanksgiving. This *is* a book about language development—the foundation of vigorous, meaningful reading and writing.

• • •

Here are ten fundamental precepts:

1. It's never too early to notice a kid's language, and it's never too late to help. Focusing on the ages mentioned above gives us a logical span for both assessment and recommendation.

2. Language develops cumulatively, its spiral joining earlier levels with new ones. Thus, parents and teachers will want to be familiar with all levels, so they can reflect on what

development has taken place and what should logically come next.

3. Gender, learning style, and heredity influence language acquisition:

- In general, females start earlier, develop language skills sooner, and throughout life are quicker at word retrieval than their male counterparts.

- People whose learning styles predispose them to hands-on, three-dimensional activities are often less interested in verbal abstraction.

- Patterns of verbal skills run in families. Children of parents who were late talkers, who are still reluctant conversationalists and readers, or who are dyslexic often inherit delayed or compromised language development. Those with strong language in the pipeline usually glom on to the nuts and bolts, shades and nuances, and rhythms and majesties of language.

We must remember these factors in both formal and informal assessment.

4. Language is made of two strands which nourish and support each other: *receptive* and *expressive*. Receptive language refers to what the child—or person of any

age—receives through listening or reading. Expressive language is that which the person puts out through speaking or writing. The relationship between the two is like that of seed and crop. What goes in determines the quality of what comes out. We are wise to keep this interdependence in mind as we notice the quality of language children absorb, just as we measure what they put out.

5. The young child *learns* language to *use*, the school-age child *uses* language to *learn*. The power in the foundation predicts the strength of the structure, thus pointing to our need to assess each child's existing language in order to set realistic expectations.

6. We can use three circles to see vital interconnections in human processes:

intellectual development   social/emotional development

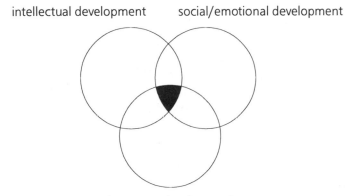

language development

From the way these intersect and overlap, it is obvious that damage or deprivation in any one will hurt the other two. Because parents and educators constantly monitor intellectual and social/emotional growth, it is easy to take language development for granted. Yet marginal or impoverished language is responsible for many of the intellectual disappointments and social/emotional misunderstandings which surround us today. Only when we know where a child's language is strong or weak can we deliver appropriate help.

7. Children climb the following rungs on the ladder of language development:

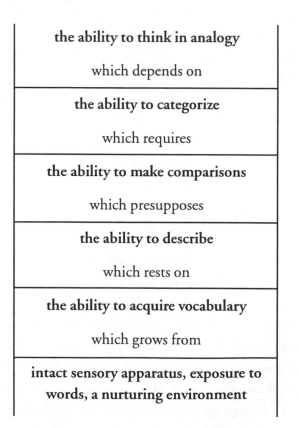

the ability to think in analogy

which depends on

the ability to categorize

which requires

the ability to make comparisons

which presupposes

the ability to describe

which rests on

the ability to acquire vocabulary

which grows from

intact sensory apparatus, exposure to words, a nurturing environment

In the good old days (if, in fact, they ever existed), teachers could assume that children would enter school with the first or lower three levels in good shape. Now, for reasons elaborated in my book *"Words Fail Me"—How Language Works and What Happens When It Doesn't*, such assumptions are perilous. Thus, we need to be familiar with the early levels on the yardstick.

8. After reading volumes of research and giving the matter my best attention, it is my view that children who are going to succeed in school and the workplace in this country need a strong base of formal English. They need to absorb its sounds, rhythms, vocabulary, and grammar. For example, as I am writing this, my young friend, Peter, and his wife, Alice, are getting ready for their trip to China to meet the Chinese-born 9-month-old girl who will become their adopted daughter. As they are making plans to nourish her with food, cuddle her with affection, and immunize her with medical miracles, I am reminding them that singing, talking, telling nursery rhymes, and speaking English parent-ese is a vital part of the life-gift they are giving Julie.

In our American tradition, communities are welcoming and absorbing families from all over the globe. As we sift through complex questions of cultural identities, we must remember that the higher rungs of the language ladder require such refinements as accurate plurals, pronouns, subject/verb agreement, verb tenses, and other markers of shading and precision. It is exactly at this level that people grappling with a new language, as well as the 20-25% of the population for whom language itself is a second language, fall apart. In giving fair shots at success to non-English speaking children (or those who are being raised by non-English speaking caregivers), we must meticulously assess where students are at the middle and high rungs of the ladder, ideally in their own tongue as well as in English. This book offers specifics.

9. Language is the key to *metacognition*, the ability to think about thinking. In this uniquely human pursuit, we harness memory, retrieval, and association. Thus aided, we channel our thoughts through *executive function*, which lets us plan, choose, and proceed, focusing our attentions, filtering out distraction, and pursuing consciously chosen goals. This requires solid language development, following the assessment continuum offered here.

10. Through language, we join the links of physical experience, emotional response, cognitive power, and abstraction in a mighty chain. Let us assess carefully to be sure children have the equipment for forging powerful links.

• • •

This book is divided into this introduction, a conclusion, a resource section, and six chapters—one apiece for the years from pre-school through fourth grade and beyond. Each chapter will:

• start with a brief overview of what we want to assess and why

- delineate probable *receptive, expressive,* and *metacognitive* language developments for that grade (Of course, the boundaries blur. Compartmentalization is but an artificial device for teasing apart the links and strands of a highly complex system.)

- highlight red flags

- suggest activities

- tell a short case history.

CHAPTER ONE

Preschool Language Assessment: What, Why, How

As we watch and listen to preschool children, what are we looking for, how do we interpret what we see and hear, what do we hope to find, what are some red flags, and why do these things matter?

Preschoolers are building the language foundations on which they will assemble the structures of their intellectual, social/emotional, and linguistic lives. Remember the three circles? Remember the ladder?

We are looking for the absence or presence of what we might call "triple lex:"

- We want to see the joy of lex—intoxication with a language system that is simultaneously malleable, flexible, sturdy, and reliable.

- We hope to see the power of lex—the ability to declare needs and feelings, ask for information, state wants, express imagination, and shuttle between the concrete and the abstract.

• We are glad to see development of lex in its *receptive*, *expressive*, and *metacognitive* aspects.

Singly and together, these propel the child on a lifelong trajectory of exploration and revelation. Let's take them in order.

Receptive language in preschool: what are we looking for, why does it matter, how do we assess?

Through the *receptive* language system, the child absorbs cadence, rhythm, vocabulary, constructions, and such different genres as bed-time stories, explanations, coaxings, admonitions, and firm prohibitions:

"... and so the little princess and the monkey went sound asleep."
"We have to go in the car because Granny is waiting."
"One more bite..."
"Be careful of the dog's ear."
"The stove is hot; don't touch."

These help the child:

• distinguish separate sounds, keeping them in proper sequence for forming words

- expand vocabulary, usually moving from concrete to picture/symbol to abstract

- taste the different linguistic flavors of conversation, questions, statements, songs, or poems

- learn new concepts: opposites, time lines, and body schema, to name a few

- label experiences and emotions to file them away for later retrieval

- absorb fact and enjoy fiction with an age-appropriate blurring of the boundary between them

- recognize and acknowledge emotion

- follow directions and explanations

- build spatial organization through the comprehension of prepositions

- organize thought with comprehension of pronouns, adjectives, and verb tenses

- distinguish separate sounds and keep them in proper sequence for forming words.

The best receptive language assessment for a preschool child is the focused attention of experienced teachers or enlightened parents. Informal assessment usually confirms the hunches of such people. Specifically, one might ask the child to:

- hold up fingers to signify age

- point to the picture of something to drink

- follow a two- or three-stage command

- identify three colors

- repeat several nonsense syllables.

If the child has trouble with any of the above, demonstrate, teach, praise, and practice, using games, manageable bites which guarantee success, and a light touch. Filter the joy, power, or difficulty of language milestones through the lex grid itemized in the lists in this chapter, using the suggested competencies as launch pads.

Expressive language in preschool: what are we looking for, why does it matter, how do we assess?

The preschool child moves from inner speech to parallel play and then to intentional, conversational involvement with others.

With inner speech, the child creates narratives and reasons to accompany or illustrate thought, play, or concerns. This inner speech, although intended solely for the benefit of its creator, may be spoken, sometimes ferociously loudly:

"Watch out! Bad guy coming! VROOOOOOOOOM! Crash." The child does not expect a rejoinder from others and, in fact, may feel ambushed if someone else tries to participate.

In parallel play, two or more children may be working in a common area, such as the block corner. They will verbalize their creations and intentions but not expect (or want) answers from others.

Finally, the child moves to conscious conversational involvement: "Here. You be the blue car; I'll be the truck." At the level of intentional conversation, the child can communicate wants, needs, ideas, questions, or, in the words of the poet Kenneth Koch, wishes, lies, and dreams.

The preschool child enjoys rhyming, making up new or nonsense words, singing songs with repetitive refrains, and telling or singing nursery rhymes. Grown-ups may say, "What's the point of nursery rhymes...they don't make sense." This is immaterial to the preschooler, who enjoys the cadences and music of the words for their own sake.

Preschool children learn to label their emotions and need to harness language to express their feelings and needs. Teaching a child to "use your words" is a lifelong tool for conveying emotions, which in turn helps the child control or direct anger, frustration, jealousy, elation, or love.

Research from the field of reading shows a powerful positive correlation between early word play and later strong reading. The best reading preparation for preschoolers is "messing around" with language—breaking words apart, making word strings, and making up new words. Adults interested in assessing the preschool child's expressive language need to listen with informed ears. Awareness leads to accurate monitoring of the child's progress on the language yardstick, as delineated above.

Metacognition in preschool: what are we looking for, why does it matter, how do we assess?

Metacognition, the ability to think about thinking, begins to develop in the preschool years, although the detachment it requires is antithetical to the immediacy of young children. Even so, signs of emergent capacities show in preschool children, particularly in two arenas: symbols and pretending.

The preschool child already knows that a word is a symbol for a person, place, or thing. The child who says "cookie" wants the real thing, not just the word. The child also learns that a picture of a cookie is a visual symbol of that delicious item, but that the picture won't taste like chocolate. This sounds so simple as to be unnecessary to discuss, but when we think of the symbolic organization and acceptance implicit in this behavior, we see that it is complex indeed. An object (a cookie), a word, and a picture all refer to the same thing, and the actual can be invoked by speech or picture.

Maturing children increase the number and complexity of symbols they understand, usually moving from the physical and concrete (*cookie, Mommy*), to the more abstract (*love*), and to such invisible, intangible abstractions as *later*.

This foundation of symbolic comprehension is the platform for understanding reading and writing. Words are symbols themselves. Words in turn are made of sounds. Letters are symbols for sounds. Letters strung together in a sequence of sounds—and cleaving to a visual shape—are symbols of words. Words strung together in print are maps of words used in speech. Thus, we complete the symbolic circle.

Unless and until children understand what symbols are and then can use them in speech and in pictures, they do not have the metacognitive underpinnings for reading and writing.

A parallel symbolic foundation is necessary for mathematics. Numeracy is the symbolic system for *how many, more, less, altogether*, etc. As we will see in the kindergarten chapter, children need to soak arbitrary symbols with personal connotation in order to lodge them in memory. In preparation, preschool children should begin counting small amounts, know how old they are, and be able to hold up the correct number of fingers to indicate their age.

As preschool children hear stories and conversation, they should be encouraged to make mental images of what they are hearing. Listening to a fairy story, they should be given time to close their eyes and imagine the princess, the giant, the troll, or the magic horse. This rapid personal translation from sound to picture—and picture to sound, emotion, and narrative—is a major building block of later solid comprehension in listening and reading. Yet it is vulnerable to theft by the ready-made images provided by TV, and by rushed situations in which adults who do not understand the importance of this invisible process hurry the child through, short-circuiting opportunities to use and increase this natural capacity.

Pretending, which looks so effortless, is actually a highly complex metacognitive exercise. For example, let's say that 3-year-old Angus wants to be a mountain lion. He has to decide what features he and a mountain lion have in common, what features of a boy are missing in a mountain lion, and what features of a mountain lion he must acquire. Then, he must cast off those boy features which would contradict his representation and put on those which are necessary to convey the "mountain lion-ness" of a mountain lion: four legs; a ferocious stance; a springy, slinking gait; a snarl; bared teeth; and stretched lips. Although these donnings and discardings are done too rapidly to be credited to conscious thought, they are part of a complex, intentional, and uniquely human process. Mountain lions don't go around trying to pretend they are boys or airplanes.

Pretending is closely allied with empathy, the ability to put oneself in another's shoes. Empathy, in turn, is the foundation of positive human relationships, as well as the ability to identify with a character in a story or a military leader in history. Empathy and language weave together in emotional growth.

The best way to assess metacognitive development in preschool children is to sit with them, telling stories, showing pictures, and seeing who "gets it" and who doesn't. Our own understanding of the roles of symbols and pretending gives us the lenses through which to view children's behavior, deciding what's on target.

Red flags

Preschool children who have trouble with *receptive* language will probably:

- be uninterested in a purely verbal story or even lose the thread of one with pictures

- have trouble following directions, often watching other children to follow the parade but being unable to lead the action themselves

- say "What?" a lot

- appear to be "in another world."

Preschool children who have problems with *expressive* language will probably:

- have trouble telling a story

- have trouble getting to the point

- have trouble negotiating, taking turns, and deciding how to share

- have trouble with "use your words."

Preschool children who have problems with *metacognition* will probably:

- prefer the concrete to the symbolic

- lose the connection between the three cookies on the plate and the words *three* or *later*

- have trouble with *what if,* as in:
  Adult: "What if it rains tomorrow when we want to have a picnic?"
  Child: "I've been in the rain."

- have trouble with the language of negotiation.

Suggested activities

Receptive language

1. Sit with the child and a picture book such as any of those written by Richard Scarry. First, talk about the items on the page and what they are called. Then, the adult can name an item and ask the child to find it. Finally, point to an item and ask the child to name it.

2. Make a set of cards by cutting strips of construction paper into pieces the size of index cards. Include as many colors as possible. Give the cards to the child or put them in

front of the child on the floor or at a desk. Pick a card. Name the color. Ask the child to match the card to some object in the room. When the child can do this comfortably, the adult says the name of a color and asks the child to find something of that color in the room. Finally, the adult points to an object and asks the child to name the color. There are, obviously, as many permutations of this as there is imagination on the part of the adult.

3. Teach, pantomime, sing, practice, and perform such simple songs as "Eensie Weensie Spider" and "I'm a Little Teapot."

The above suggestions help children connect words to their experiences.

Expressive language

1. Sit with the child and look over any one of the vast collection of wordless books. (Any librarian can help you find a stack of them.) First, look through the pictures together, naming some of the obvious items. Then, go back to the beginning and ask the child to tell the story of what is happening. Stick to the sequence in the book.

2. Sit with the child and the same Richard Scarry book (or a different one), but this time let the child practice naming the various objects and creatures that Scarry so meticulously offers.

3. Get a small collection of puppets. It doesn't matter whether they are animals or people. Ask the child to have the

puppet enact such activities of daily living as brushing teeth, combing hair, and putting on shoes, but ask the child to let the puppet use words to describe what is happening.

These activities help children frame their actions in words.

Metacognition

1. Play simple games of Lotto, first asking the child simply to match the cards to the pictures on the game board. Then, the adult can follow the sequence delineated above: identify, match, select, name.

2. "Talking-walking" involves strolling with the child through the room, down the hall, or out-of-doors. The location doesn't matter. The object is to notice, name, and talk about what the child sees. Insofar as possible, encourage the child to use labels, attributes (*sharp, fuzzy, green*), and functions (for keeping your feet dry, for cutting paper, for drinking). Prompt this by asking a readily manageable number of questions: "Yes, this a water fountain. How do we use it?"

3. Play finger-counting games: "Show me one finger...show me three fingers...show me one finger and three fingers at the same time—how many fingers altogether?"

These activities help connect words, actions, and thinking.

Case study

Throughout this book, we will follow the fortunes of a pair of fraternal twins, Francine and Adam, born to loving parents who had faced the disappointments of infertility.

With medical help, a successful pregnancy resulted in the late-summer births of full-term, healthy, normal twins.

Each baby is a miracle, but sometimes when parents have been discouraged and frightened, an actual living, breathing baby (or, in this case, two) can cause overwhelming happiness. Miraculously, these parents resisted the temptation to spoil the babies, who grew through their infancies with love, trust, firm boundaries, humor, stories, books, blocks, and dolls.

In early childhood, Adam was a man of action who preferred building with blocks to hanging around listening to stories. Although small for his age, he enjoyed playground activities with other children and was particularly, energetically imaginative. His rendition of Batman brought the world right into Gotham City. Gleefully, he would turn himself from Batman into an airplane, a ferocious animal, or a king.

Adam and Francine got along well, perhaps because they were so different. Francine was tiny, meticulously tidy, physically cautious, and verbally precocious. In her early childhood, she liked to play house. She tended her stuffed animals with great responsibility and affection, soaked up stories, and would retell whole sections of them later in linguistic wax impressions. Her parents would often hear her in her room giving her toy rabbit a verbatim rendition of a story she had just heard for the first time. She learned the names of colors, body parts, and exotic foods—all with great ease—

13

and would use them in conversation. At age four, she said, "I think couscous has better flavor than pasta."

The parents were extremely careful in choosing the twins' preschool. They visited several, asked intelligent questions, and reflected on the answers and on what they saw. Having made their choice, they applied, and Adam and Francine were accepted. The twins started their education even though their late summer birthday fell after the standard admissions cut-off date. (The children seemed eager and relatively mature, the parents were enthusiastic, and the school had two openings in the class.) Starting school, albeit a bit early, seemed both normal and wise.

Children are full of surprises.

CHAPTER TWO

Kindergarten Language Assessment: What, Why, How

Kindergarten is a year of linguistic and cognitive explosion. How do these work together? What can we expect? What building blocks are developing and what does their presence or absence imply?

As kindergartners incorporate the elements mentioned in the introductory part of Chapter One, they also break new ground. As younger children need to *learn* the language of negotiation to develop their social skills, kindergartners *exercise* their negotiation skills with ever increasing verbal fluency and persuasive powers.

Receptive language widens and deepens its receptacles. *Expressive* language grows more robust. *Metacognitive* skills move into vital areas of sorting. Let's see how.

Receptive language in kindergarten: what are we looking for, why does it matter, how do we assess?

As *receptive* language capacities increase, they allow the child to concentrate for longer periods of time, to pay closer attention to narrative or factual details, to make increasingly wide associations, and to remember and file what they are taking in with increasing efficiency. This, of course, allows for greater power in retrieval and the subsequent ability to make novel connections and think up original projects and ideas.

Most kindergarten children:

- comprehend pronouns and such regular and irregular plurals as *dogs* and *mice*

- understand regular and irregular verb tenses: *land/ landed* and *stand/ stood, (standed* being a highly intelligent error)

- have an internal time line on which to travel from present to recent past and distant past, and thence to logical anticipation of the future (Kindergarten children separate those time zones conceptually, although they join them in the ribbon of personal history.)

- understand such sense shifters as *unless, until,* and above all, *if*

- grasp the implications of behavior control through such words as *later* and *next*

- can digest and execute a three-part command ("Go to the door, jump three times, say your name.")

- are able to break apart familiar words into chunks and reassemble them with parts missing ("Say *nutmeg*...say it again but leave out *meg*." See Rosner's *Helping Children Overcome Learning Difficulties*. Capacities for this kind of phonemic segmentation are proving to be vital reading readiness skills.)

- are learning that conversation is a ping-pong game in which people listen as well as talk.

Here are 8 quick ways to assess a kindergartner's prowess. Spend five minutes talking with the child alone. Then:

- After playing with the concept of plurals, give the child six nouns, one at a time, and ask him or her to say the plural. Suggested words might be: *shoe, knife, belt, candy, kiss, hand.*

- Next, do the same with verbs, providing present tense and asking for past tense: *jump, eat, scratch, bring.* (Like *standed* or *stooded, branged* is a brilliant error, showing fundamental but misapplied grasp of the pattern.)

- Next, draw a line perhaps 11 inches long. In the middle, put a dot, saying, "We're going to use this line to describe your life. This dot in the middle is where you and I are right now. On this side (the left), we'll put things that happened in the past. On this side (the right), we'll put things that will happen in the future. Can you show me where you would put the day you were born, or your next birthday, or last summer. Are there any things you would like to put on the line?"

- *Unless, until* and *if* are the underpinnings of the old parlor game, Simon Says. Play a round or two. See who gets it and who goofs up.

- Give the child a three-part command to hear, remember, and execute: "Pick up a pencil, *next* drop it on the floor, and *later* put it back on the table."

- Play a set of the phonemic segmentation exercises in Rosner's book, or make up some different ones such as, "Say *printer*...say it again but leave out *er*...say *feet*...say it again but leave out /f/...say *feet*...say it again but leave out /t/ ...say *trap*...say it again but leave out /r/." Most kindergartners would be able to do the first three, but many would stumble on the final one.

• Finally, talk with the child about a subject interesting to him or her. Does the conversation go back and forth like ping-pong?

Expressive language in kindergarten: what are we looking for, why does it matter, how do we assess?

The linguistically intact kindergarten child is learning to:

• formulate a question (It is likely that we are the only species on the planet with this capability.)

• use correct regular and irregular plurals, with a few lapses for the type of smart errors listed above

• use pronouns accurately

• use verb tenses accurately (Use bespeaks comprehension.)

• have subject/verb agreement in most instances

• put events in reliable sequence/plot:
  starting with personal events
  moving to recounting a story
  moving to projecting likely events

• attach words to original art work

• create stories

• retrieve familiar words rapidly and efficiently.

To find out where children are with these developing capabilities, listen to them, noticing whether they incorporate the verbal skills listed above.

Word retrieval is an especially important area for assessment, because children with slow, arrhythmic, or inefficient word retrieval systems are likely to be slow, hesitant, and frequently reluctant readers. Rudel and Denckla invented a short word retrieval test that a teacher can make easily. You need a grid of twenty-five squares and simple line drawings of five common objects. Examples might include: *pencil, book, candle, telephone, mug.* Scatter the drawings randomly in the grid, so that each object appears five times, but the objects and the rows do not repeat.

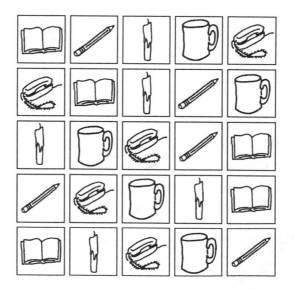

Tell the student you are going to ask him or her to run a little "talking race." Rehearse the first line of the grid, which should include each of the objects, to be sure the child knows what the items are called. Then say, "I'm going to ask you to go through my chart as quickly as you can, saying the name of each picture. I'm going to time you to see how quickly and correctly you can do it. Ready, get set, go."

Start timing as the child says the first word, keep track of errors, and count the time in seconds. A collection of ten, twenty, or thirty scores will provide a range of performance for a particular school, and make it easy to see who is swift and who is pokey. The reason this matters is that skillful reading requires readers' rapid retrieval of words from their own internal language pool, in order to match them up with the squiggles on the page called printed words.

Metacognition in kindergarten: what are we looking for, why does it matter, how do we assess?

In the course of the kindergarten year, most children begin to develop and then solidify four abilities which they subsequently need for formal academic learning:

- the ability to sit still and concentrate

- the ability to learn and manipulate symbols

- the ability to postpone gratification

• the ability to distinguish between reality and
   fantasy.

As the reality/fantasy boundary solidifies, children can
stabilize their universes, knowing whether something is likely
or unlikely. When they can make this determination, they
can distinguish between funny, scary, slapstick, and genu-
inely perilous. Until then, if *anything* can happen, *everything*
has a dangerous edge.

Kindergartners also refine and polish their ability to recognize and create rhymes, and to play with *onomatopoeia*
—when the sound a word makes also conveys its meaning
(the *buzzing* of the bees). Hyla Rubin, who enchants count-
less kindergartners with her humor and her games, likes to
use the book *There's a Rocket in My Pocket* to encourage rhyming with new, made-up words and the enjoyment of the
ludicrous.

She also encourages children to bring their favorite
stuffed animal to school. The children sit in a circle and introduce their animals. Then, she asks the children to work in
pairs, combining the name or species of their animals. For
example, one child has an *elephant*, another a *hippopotamus*.
Combined, they turn up an *elepotamus* and a *hippophant*.
Next, she asks the children to imagine how a *hippophant* is
different from an *elephant* or a *hippopotamus*, and then do the
same with the *elepotamus*. Finally, she asks the children to
introduce the newly minted animals to each other, ascribing
habits and preferences to each of the imaginary creatures.

The only outer limit to this kind of exploration is the teacher's imagination.

To assess kindergartner's metacognition, we need to observe their daily behavior, looking for the absence or presence of the four abilities, and the children's delight in and understanding of such word play as rhyming, onomatopoeia, and creating and playing with nonsense words and syllables. No formal test is as accurate as the informed ear of an adult who cares.

Red flags

Kindergartners who have trouble with *receptive* language will probably:

- have trouble carrying out three-part commands

- mis-sequence sounds or syllables in words they speak: eating a *hangaburger*, reading a *mazagine*, or seeing an *ephelant* at the circus (All children make such errors from time to time. Frequency is the tip-off.)

- exhibit impulsivity, since they do not govern their own behavior through such language as *after, before, unless, until,* or *whenever*

- interrupt or tune-out in conversation more frequently than their peers.

Kindergartners who have trouble with *expressive* language will probably:

- have arrhythmic speech—halting, rushed, or filled with such imprecisions and time buyers as "the um...you know...thingy"

- use imprecise or incorrect sequence in stories or events they are trying to relate

- tangle pronouns, forget plural endings, or use or omit incorrect verb tense endings

- use inflection instead of syntax in forming a question. ("The dog is gone?")

Kindergartners who have trouble with *metacognition* will probably:

- have trouble inventing an imaginary tale

- have trouble putting dialogue in the mouth of a puppet

- live in the moment

- mix up reality and fantasy.

Suggested activities

Receptive language

1. With a single child or small group, play the game of Simon Says, referred to on page 18. As a review of the rules, the teacher explains that the children will be given com-

mands one at a time. They are to listen but carry out the command *only* if it is preceded by the words "Simon says." For example, "Simon Says tap your foot," means the children are to do so. After three or four commands carefully preceded by "Simon says," the teacher should give a command such as, "Clap your hands." Oops! It was not preceded by the magic words, so the children should have done nothing. For this age, avoid eliminating children who make mistakes. They take games seriously and get hurt feelings.

2. Get or make a bag roughly half the size of a pillow case. A paper shopping bag works well. Then, assemble a group of familiar objects, such as a lipstick, a comb, a sponge, a shoelace, a pen, etc. Show these to the children and have them practice naming and describing them. Then, put the objects in "The Feely Bag" and ask a child with eyes closed or averted to reach in the bag and "find something slippery" or "find something bendable" or "find something hard." Use your imagination to invent the commands, Just be sure there is something in the bag that fills the bill.

3. Ask the children to sit down and close their eyes. Tell them you are going to read a poem aloud, and they are to turn their minds into a screen on which they will project the images in the poem. After the reading, ask them to open their eyes and either draw or describe one of their own images. There are endless excellent anthologies of children's poetry available. Any librarian or fellow teacher can make recommendations.

These activities help children focus on incoming words.

Expressive language

1. Children who have trouble with word retrieval may profit from an "Is It...Or Is It...Visit." The teacher takes a picture book (I have already mentioned my favorite author, Richard Scarry, but there are millions of others on the market) and points to an item or a person, saying, "What is this?" or "What is this person called?" If the child answers correctly, well and good. Move on to harder items until the child is stumped.

Let's imagine the teacher has pointed to a picture of a plumber. The teacher says, "Let's play an Is It...Or Is It...Visit. Is it a bus driver or is it a 'pl...'" In most instances, the simple prompt of the first two letters will nudge the child's retrieval: "Oh, yes! It's a plumber!" The teacher should then reinforce the word by repeating it and exchanging a few sentences with the child using the newly retrieved word. This strategy provides endless practice in a light-hearted yet productive fashion.

2. The teacher collects a group of puppets and tells the child he or she is going to create a theater of experiences. The child chooses a puppet, and the teacher asks the child to be the voice of the puppet describing an ordinary activity or experience. For example, "Please let your puppet tell about getting up this morning and having something to eat." Encourage the child to put events in sequence, notice and reinforce correct use of verb tenses, and let imagination soar.

3. Return to the Feely Bag. Ask children, one at a time, to put a hand in the bag, grasp one of the objects, and describe it using two attributes. For example, "This is something stiff and as long as my finger." The others guess. In this instance, the example refers to the lipstick.

These exercises help children deliver language.

Metacognition

1. Revisit the Feely Bag. Ask children to take a turn finding the object the teacher is thinking of. The teacher describes the object by opposites. For example "Find something which is the opposite of soft." Of course there can be many correct answers to questions posed in this way.

2. Arrange a collection of magnetic letters in alphabetical order. Then, give children a turn by saying, "I'm going to say a word to you. I want you to find the letter that makes the first sound in my word, and the letter that makes the last sound in my word." Use any words that come to mind. This is *not* primarily a lesson in reading. Rather, it is an exercise to practice sound segmentation—a *foundation* of reading.

3. The teacher shows children how to make a set of Traffic Light cards by cutting slips of construction paper in red, green, and orange. The teacher explains that she is going to say a word, and then name a sound from that word. If the sound is in the beginning of the word, the children should hold up the green card. If the sound is at the end of the word, they should hold up the red card. If it is in the middle of the

word, they should hold up the orange card. An example might be: "My word is *tap*, my sound is /t/," or "My word is *tap*, my sound is /p/," or "My word is *tap*, my sound is /a/." Again, this is practice in a *foundation* of reading—knowing where sounds are located within words.

These exercises help children attach their thinking to the language with which they are surrounded.

Case study

In kindergarten, Francine was a well-groomed little girl, who—even in this era of blue jeans, tights, and tunics—liked to wear dresses and ribbons in her hair. With the exception of her twin, Adam, she tended to be more comfortable with grown-ups than with children her own age. Because she was companionable as well as beautiful, she received a great deal of attention from the adults in her world. She had been read to, talked with, and sung to throughout her childhood, and because she was a good mimic and remembered facts easily, she appeared to be very advanced. She had been able to name the days of the week, identify colors, maintain good crayon control, thread beads, cut, and paste. In short, she had taken in a great deal of information through her *receptive* system, and given out volumes of correct information through her *expressive* system. Her verbal facility created an illusion of a highly advanced intellectual level. Some adults wondered whether she shouldn't be accelerated.

Fortunately for Francine, her grandmother was skeptical, saying, "I'm so glad I live nearby. I love being with her. She likes to play in my button box and help me cook, but she doesn't like to get messy in the kitchen, she gets fretful if someone challenges her, she doesn't like to play and pretend with other children, and when something isn't quite right, she panics. Days of the week? Flawless! Frustration or uncertainty? She can't cope. I'd hate to see her leapfrog ahead into a curriculum where she'd be learning letters and numbers but not having the chances to *play with* and *use* her knowledge. What good is information if you can't toss it up in the air, make new ideas, and use it with enjoyment? I think she needs more time to let her thinking catch up with her information."

Action-oriented Adam adored the playground. Swinging from bars, "leaping tall buildings at a single bound," skipping, climbing, and jumping, he was joyfully alive when using his body. His spatial sense was as uncanny as that of a cat—he knew just where he could fit himself. He enjoyed playing with the other children even though he was small and younger than most of the other boys, sometimes by as much as nine months to a year. He was also younger than all the girls in his class, and since girls are linguistically more advanced than boys in the early years, the gap between him and the members of the opposite sex seemed enormous.

Intelligence and imagination showed in his Lego creations and legendary stories. His supply of general information put him way out in front, and yet he had a long, hard struggle to learn letter names and sounds, and he still grew very confused by the sight of numbers. His pencil was more of a saboteur than an ally, and though energetic in play situations, he yawned deeply and frequently when asked to sit and work at his desk-table.

Near the end of kindergarten, he still had none of the four abilities previously mentioned in this chapter's section on metacognition: he was not ready to sit still and concentrate, he couldn't remember symbols and had no grasp of why they mattered, he couldn't postpone gratification, and he interwove reality and fantasy in a warp and woof of magic carpet.

Even so, his father said, "But we *must* send him on to first grade. It will make a man of him."

The teacher said, "How about letting him be a little boy on his way to becoming a man? When we look ahead to third and fourth grades and higher, we find a large percentage of the kids who are having trouble are boys with late summer birthdays. It is also true that boys who have trouble mastering pens and pencils may wing it during first and second grades, but when they need to join motor and mental skills in third grade, the ones with small-motor problems frequently become disproportionately discouraged. Why risk it? For what? It would be such a shame to let his shiny eyes, eagerness, intelligence, and motor abilities disguise his need for another year to play, grow up, and refine his receptive, expressive, and metacognitive skills. He could let them shine, ripe and ready, the following year."

"This wouldn't be coddling?" the father asked.

"No", said the teacher, "It would be giving him the chance to be a legitimately hard worker when he's ready for the tasks which would be set out for him."

"What about Francine?" the parents asked. "It would be wrong to have one go ahead and the other be left back."

The teacher said "Francine would benefit from an extra year, too. And let's not say 'left back;' how about saying 'given time?'"

"But they both seem so bright. What's gone wrong?"

"Nothing's gone wrong," said the teacher. "I just want to subtract twelve days from their ages and give them a new birthday: July 31. Our school cut-off date is August 1, as you know. If their real birthdays were July 31, would you be having a hard time with this decision? No? Then please, as a present to me, pretend to subtract these few days, and I promise you will be adding geometrically to both their lives, now and in all the years to come."

The twins received "the gift of time." During the second year in kindergarten, Adam had ample chances to play and to develop the four metacognitive competencies listed above. Francine spent two afternoons a week in a low-key, after-school arts and drama program, and was encouraged by her grandmother to illustrate the stories she heard and to increase by tenfold her use of the words *why* and *because*. Time gave both children a chance to grow in the different directions their natures needed.

CHAPTER THREE

First Grade Language Assessment: What, Why, How

As students master print in first grade, they join the language in their lives to the words they see or write in print. Some children, though, have trouble getting going. Some have trouble learning sound/symbol correspondence; many can't remember sight words and suffer in Whole Language programs. Many of the children who struggle with the early mechanical levels of reading don't understand the purpose. They don't know that letters represent sounds, and that strings of letters represent words, and that words strung together make sentences.

Asked "What is reading?" three first graders answered:
"So everybody has to be quiet."
"When my Mom and Dad sit in the newspaper."
"Finding out anything you want."

Receptive language, *expressive* language, and *metacognition* interweave ever more closely in the first grade child. Let's see how.

Receptive language in first grade: what are we looking for, why does it matter, how do we assess?

Receptive language is made up of both listening and reading. Whether children are listening to a poem read aloud or attending to directions or instructions, they need to make their own mental images to accompany what they are hearing. As mentioned in previous sections, many of today's children are unpracticed, having learned to depend on TV to provide the images for them.

As they exercise their "mind's eye" in listening, children this age launch themselves on their reading careers. They explore the mysteries and excitement of decoding—knowing the sounds each letter makes and stringing the sounds together to make words from the printed squiggles. It is vital for adults to remember that children this age enjoy decoding for its own sake. They are like little James Bonds, each minuscule 007 mastering the code. Sometimes, grown-ups forget this and assume children would find such exercises either boring or demeaning. But in fairness to children, we have to remember the power of natural appetites and provide children with chances to do what they think is fun.

At the height of the Whole Language craze, I had a call from a mother of a child mid-way through first grade. This little boy had been surrounded by stories and language since birth, his home was filled with books, his parents spent quality time with him, and he was attending an extremely prestigious school. The mother called me in tears, saying, "I don't know what to do with Ned. He's crabby and unhappy. He's making life miserable for his little brother as well as for his father and me. I couldn't figure out what was wrong until he fell apart this morning when I asked him to stop picking on his brother, be quiet, and just read the cereal box. That did it. He smacked the cereal box onto the floor and dissolved. 'That's just the trouble' he wailed. 'I can't even read the cereal box! In school they tell me I'm learning to read, but that isn't true. I listen to the stories and kind of sing along with the teacher, but I don't know how to read. I'll NEVER know how to read.'"

"What are we going to do?" wept the mother to me.

"We're going to TEACH him to read," I said. "I'll smuggle you some phonics materials, and you use them to show him how to read."

Three months later, the child called me, saying, "I read a whole book. I read it all myself. Do you want to come over so I can read it to you? It's all about baseball." On my way to his house, I assumed from his pride that it was some sort of statistical tome. Imagine my surprise when he greeted me with an 8-page copy of a beginning reader called *Jim Wins*. The child read it page by page—"Jim will win. Jim will hit it."—all the way to the denouement on page 8—"Jim wins!" I think the real winner was the reader!

As children master reading, they harness many strategies: they use phonics to decode, they use visual memory to recognize sight words, they use inference to guess what words are coming next, they use context clues and pictures to give themselves a shot at an unfamiliar word, and they use emerging comprehension skills to keep knitting the story together. To do all this, children integrate muscle movements, memory, general information, and their own internal pools of language. Reading is a highly integrative process whose success depends on strong language foundations. Thus, in assessing first grader's language, we look for the absence or presence of the above skills.

Here's a folk truth to remember when a child has trouble catching on to reading. Many times, children who have not yet lost their baby teeth have trouble integrating the pre-reading skills of letter recognition, etc., into the process of real reading. We teach, we tutor, we try harder, but still the skills don't coalesce. One fine day, out falls a baby tooth, then another, and the new teeth are ready to drop down. It has long been my experience that the tooth fairy brings more than a dime (or a dollar, these days); the tooth fairy can bring readiness to read. It's as though the loss of baby teeth is a visible symptom of an internal maturation, and one of the results may be readiness for real reading.

Nonsense words are an ideal way to assess the accuracy of a child's decoding skills. Here are ten samples (in appropriate categories) to ask the child to read:

- consonant/vowel/consonant: *fam, des, lin, pof, suf*

- consonant/vowel/consonant blend at the beginning: *brin*

- consonant/vowel/consonant blend at the end: *gamp*

- consonant blend/vowel/consonant blend: *blist*

- silent *e*: *gade*

- vowel team: *beag*

Similarly, invent some nonsense sight words for children to see, learn, remember, and read: *stasha, bleasness, faioul, reester, kyrist.*

Why do this? A child who can decode nonsense words can decode real words. Using nonsense words, you are sure the child is decoding instead of recognizing. In addition, errors are arrows to areas of confusion. Locate the trouble and teach what the child needs.

Also, test first grader's ability to count the number of sounds in a word. Only if they can do that will they know how many letters that word uses—vital information for reading or writing. Try *cat, lap, lamp, lamps* for starters.

Expressive language in first grade: what are we looking for, why does it matter, how do we assess?

Through *expressive* language—speaking and writing—a first grader should be able to:

- tell a story

- recount an event

- continue a story from someone else's beginning

- describe a person, place, or thing

- use correct verb tenses, plurals, and pronouns

- make strings of alliteration.

First graders are ready (and willing!) to have daily dictation exercises. (See my book *Common Ground*, listed in the resource section.) Through this process, they hear a word, repeat it aloud, analyze it, and write it. First graders progress from single sounds to single words, to short phrases, to sentences, and finally to incomplete sentences or story starters that they finish.

Here are examples of each. Let's say the class is working on the short sound of the vowel *u*. The teacher would begin by introducing the sound, writing the letter on the board, illustrating its correct position on the line, and asking the children to brainstorm some words containing that sound.

The teacher would write those words on the board and leave them there as reference points. Then, the teacher would ask the children to take out pencil and paper, write their names on their papers, and listen for the dictation.

"I'm going to say a sound. You listen, say it out loud, and write the letter that makes my sound: /u/."

"Good. Now I'm going to say a word which has that sound. Listen to my word, say it out loud, and write it out one sound at a time. My word is *cut.*"

"Fine. Let's try three more words." The teacher would give them slowly, as in the above example, perhaps using: *sup, mug, gut.*

"Great going. Now I'm going to give you a phrase. Listen to it, repeat it, count the number of words in my phrase, and write each one." (Remember to leave spaces between words: *in the tub, dug it up,* and so forth.)

"We're whizzing along. Now, here's my sentence: *I am in the mud.*"

"Now, here's a sentence for me to start and for you to finish. I'll say my part. You count how many words I have said, write them, and finish the sentence any way you want. For the part you are going to make up, you can use any words you like. Try your best to spell them by sounding them out, and if you need help, ask me. After you are through, please illustrate what you have written. Here we go: *It is fun to...*"

For ready-made word lists, consult *Recipe For Reading* in the resource section or compile your own.

Of course, what a child can write from your dictation—or dictation from his or her own head, which is what creative writing is—is not a full measure of the child's expressive language capacity. The integration of motor skills with thinking is still rudimentary. But when we listen to what children can tell us, being aware of the elements discussed in the first part of this section, and then look at what they can write either with help or spontaneously, we see and hear their comfort and facility with sound/symbol correspondence and the overall processes of language.

Metacognition in first grade: what are we looking for, why does it matter, how do we assess?

First graders need to know that language is made of words, which are symbols for people, places, or things, and that print is a symbol for those symbols. Language—written or spoken—is the symbol system through which people can share and communicate. First grade children must have the gut-level understanding of what symbols are in order to understand reading and writing. They need to have accumulated this concept as suggested in the pre-school chapter. Then, they need to develop such rich webs of connotations that they can readily recall the meaning of those symbols from memory.

Neurologists refer to *convergence zones*—mental areas (which I think of in the imagery of a table) to which a thinker brings:

- the present stimulus

- past knowledge and associations

- tangential ideas

and mixes them together in original thinking.

Multi-sensory teaching, which simultaneously harnesses visual, auditory, motor, language, and emotional systems, helps even the most recalcitrant student bring those arbitrary symbols we call letters and numerals into the matrix of personal growth, skill development, and imagination.

Using *metacognition*, the linguistically intact and ready first grader will be able to:

- join comprehension to decoding, moving from "barking at print" to absorbing meaning

- extend the delight of pretending from the body involvement of pantomime to the abstraction of telling or writing a story

- map speech onto print

- understand the symbolic function of numbers and be able to travel a tangible or mental number line, adding, subtracting, and seeing intervals

- use manipulatives to illustrate what numbers represent.

Thus, in the *metacognitive* realm, we hope to see the awareness of symbols that allows the child to make sense of those mechanical processes of reading and writing the adult world takes so seriously. Sadly, many children whose language is under-cultivated are being exhorted by zealous, earnest teachers to learn things whose function they do not grasp, and to engage in the seemingly pointless actions of turning squiggles into sounds, and shapes into spoken words. The best way to assess the absence or presence of such metacognition is for adults to understand these processes themselves and then spend time with the child who is reading, writing, and working. There is no substitute for the watchful eye of an enlightened, loving grown-up.

Red flags

If first graders of average or above intelligence who have intact sensory apparatus—and who are being taught with methods and materials that work for their peers—still do not latch on to the symbols of written language, they need an individual assessment designed to detect dyslexia or other learning disabilities.

The child who has trouble with phonemic segmentation (see earlier sections) is headed for trouble in decoding and encoding.

Obviously, the child whose vocabulary is small from lack of exposure is at risk for reading.

Children cannot repeat from memory a sentence construction more elaborate than one they could invent themselves. Therefore, a test of sentence memory gives a window into both *receptive* and *expressive* language levels. There are many commercially available tests, but here are three sentences the linguistically intact child should manage to repeat verbatim in first grade. Try them and see who can and cannot.

I have two feet.
Betsy wants to get a dog biscuit for her puppy.
John has eaten a bowl of sweet peaches with his little sister.

Children who stumble over the Rapid Automatic Naming described in the previous chapter, or whose speech is littered with such fillers and time buyers as "and...um" or "thingy," will probably have parallel difficulties with rhythmic word recall in reading.

Children whose articulation and speech patterns are arrhythmic may have parallel problems in the fine motor process of writing. Speaking is the motor component of *verbal* expressive language; handwriting is the motor component of *written* expressive language. Those with hesitant or faltering motor control will usually have similar difficulties in each of these two domains. The $64,000 term for this is *grapho-motor-bocca-lingual link*, which, when we break it apart, is a very simple word. *Grapho* refers to writing, *motor* refers to muscle power and coordination, *bocca* means mouth, and *lingua* refers to tongue. The connection to the word *language* is too obvious to belabor.

First graders who have trouble with *metacognition* usually:

- have trouble following spoken or written directions

- can memorize number combinations but can't think creatively with numbers (They are more comfortable with the answers of arithmetic than the questions of mathematics.)

- struggle to invent alternative endings to stories

- may cling to one friend because they lack the negotiation skills to be a real part of the group.

Suggested activities

Receptive language

1. Play Simon Says at a more difficult level. For a review of the rules, see the preceding chapter. This time, the teacher tells the children they are going to hear two commands each time. They are to listen hard and only do them if they are preceded by the words "Simon Says." The teacher might say,

"Simon Says clap your hands and then touch your toes," or "Simon Says first scratch your ear and then lift up your left foot," or "Simon Says before you lift up your left foot, touch your knee," or "Touch your knee and then wiggle your thumb." Gotcha!

2. Here is an age-appropriate way for children to respond to hearing poetry read aloud. The teacher reads the poem aloud. The children listen with closed eyes. Then, they take turns saying a word or phrase they heard in the poem.

3. Some children who have trouble *decoding* nonsense words may need to practice *encoding* them. The teacher spreads the magnetic letters out in alphabetical order and then says, "We are going to practice building some nonsense words. After we have built them, we'll read them together. The first word we're going to build is *nug*. What's the first sound you hear in *nug*? Good. You're right. Find the *n* and put it in front of you. What's the next sound you hear?" and so forth. When the word is built, teacher and student practice reading it together. Somehow, the experience of physically moving letters around turns on the light for some kids.

These activities help children clarify and remember the language around them.

Expressive language

1. Using a collection of puppets, tell the child that he or she is going to create a "theater of feelings." (The preceding chapter used experiences.) The child takes a puppet, and the

teacher says, "Please let your puppet say something that would help in making friends...Yes, 'May I play, too?' is a very good way to make friends. Now let your puppet say something that would express happiness..." and so forth. Putting feelings into words is a vital skill. Shy or reluctant children will often speak powerfully through the protection of a puppet.

2. Something Old, Something New is a way to prompt word play and imagination. In the preceding chapter, we saw Hyla Rubin's game of putting animal species together. This builds on that foundation. The teacher asks each child to think of five common objects. The teacher writes the words on the board, and draws a little picture to accompany each one. Or, the teacher may use the objects from the Feely Bag. Each child takes a turn putting a piece of one label with a piece of another. For example the child might name a pencil and a pillow, and put them together to make a *pen-low*. Then, the child has to say how it would be used. An answer might be, "A pen-low is what you use to write a bedtime story." The teacher should ask the children to make illustrations of their new creations.

3. The teacher can help the children build a word bank organized by initial consonant. Ideally, the activity will begin by isolating one letter, then brainstorming as many words as the group can think of which begin with that letter. The teacher writes the words on a piece of poster board. The next day, the group chooses another letter and repeats the proce-

dure. Each word bank stays on the wall to be added to as inspiration strikes.

These activities are designed to foster expressive word play.

Metacognition

1. Here is a more complex and abstract way to use the Feely Bag. The teacher may stick with the objects already collected, or use them with several additions, or simply start from scratch. Then, the teacher asks the child to select an item not by its property or opposite, as suggested earlier, but by its function. For example, "Find something you would use in the kitchen," (a spatula) or "Find something you would need if you were wrapping a present," (scissors).

2. The teacher gives each child a set of magnetic letters and asks him or her to arrange the letters in alphabetical order. Then, as a way of practicing cardinal and ordinal numbers, she asks the child to "Identify the seventh letter," or "Give the sound of the fourteenth letter," or "Show me the third letter from the end," or "Put the sound of two letters together," or "Take five letters away and count how many are left."

3. The teacher gives each child a set of upper-case magnetic letters and also a set of lower-case letters, asking him or her to match them up.

These activities help children catalogue language and information together.

Case study

Because each child's behavior and preference pattern was so distinct, because they were so different from each other, and because twins are noticeable, people categorized and predicted how Adam and Francine would perform in school.

"Gifted," was whispered about Francine. "All boy...very nice," was said of Adam.

In first grade, Adam had trouble staying at his work table. He took many of what Jim Grant calls "in-house field trips"—traveling to the bathroom, the nurse, the water fountain, his cubby, a friend's work station, etc. He had trouble remembering what sounds the letters made, his handwriting was large and irregular, and he would gaze longingly at the jungle gym.

Francine was in paradise. She kept her pencils nicely sharpened, never tore the paper off her crayons, relished the workbook pages she was offered, remembered sight words easily, and was in The Bluebirds reading group. She learned her number combinations quickly, and by Thanksgiving had memorized her pairs from 2+2 all the way through 12+12.

It seemed clear that she would be an exceptional student and that Adam would galumph along behind her.

Isn't life strange?

CHAPTER FOUR

Second Grade Language Assessment: What, Why, How

Contrary to common belief, children don't "get" language from reading; rather, they "get" reading from language. They must have the vocabulary, cadence, rhythm, and constructions inside for print to be meaningful and to reverberate. Children who have been raised on verbal fast food—the Golden Arches of McLanguage—haven't developed enough language to make reading meaningful, let alone pleasant or compelling.

Second graders are busy integrating the pre-reading and early reading skills they have tried to master in pre-school, kindergarten, and first grade. As their new teeth emerge, their articulation becomes increasingly accurate, and they usually develop easy congress between what they hear, read, speak, and say. In school, they are still in a period of great receptivity and excitement about the decoding/encoding process. Their *receptive* language capacity expands, soaking up new vocabulary in many and varying realms. Their *expressive* language expands on paper as well as verbally. And their *metacognition* expands in factual foundations of general information, and an ever-increasing ability to manage such abstractions as time and the beginnings of formal reading comprehension techniques. Let's look at some of the particulars.

Receptive language in second grade: what are we looking for, why does it matter, how do we assess?

Receptive language, as we know from the previous section, refers to both listening and reading. The ready second grader, whose language is intact, absorbs new information, ideas, and concepts in fact, fiction, phonemic awareness, mathematics, and figurative language. Specifically, most second graders:

- know the names of most of their body parts, including such terms as *thigh* or *collar bone*

- are eager to learn the scientific vocabulary of weather, volcanos, other cultures, the arts, or music (One second grader said, "Do you want to see me dance *andante* or *presto?*")

- are able to follow three-step directions or explanations ("Here's how we're going to do our project. You will need a pair of scissors, three felt-tip markers in different colors, and a

handful of paper clips. Please get them now." It
helps to have visuals as reminders.)

- can blend separated sounds into words—they
can convert "c-a-t" into *cat*, "d-r-o-p" into
drop, "d-e-s-k" into *desk*, "t-r-a-m-p" into
tramp, "but-ter-fly" into *butterfly*, "sen-sa-tion-
al" into *sensational*, or "con-grat-u-la-tions"
into *congratulations* (Of course, in order to do
this they need to know the words to begin
with.)

- can separate words into sounds and count how
many sounds need to be represented by letters

- enjoy hearing chapter books read aloud; can
tolerate the interruption of stopping and
continuing; remember the plot, characters,
and details; and enjoy mulling over the story
and wondering what's coming next

- feel superior to such characters as Amelia
Bedelia, who—when asked to dust the
furniture—opens the vacuum cleaner bag and
sprinkles dust on the tables and chairs
(Enjoyment of this type of humor shows an
emergent ability to endow single words with
multiple meanings.)

- like to break apart compound words, understanding the derivation of such words as *handbag* and trying to make sense of *sandwich*

- begin to feel at home with figures of speech. (Most of them know that "It's raining cats and dogs" doesn't mean that animals are dropping out of the sky.)

Children who cannot do these things are showing us they are below expected levels on the language yardstick. They need simple exercises to refine these fundamental skills. It is an easy matter to use this list of skills as a springboard to planning games and activities.

Expressive language in second grade: what are we looking for, why does it matter, how do we assess?

Expressive language refers to both speaking and writing. Most second graders enjoy:

- retelling or inventing stories with sequenced plots

- making story boards, cartoon frames, or dioramas or collages as illustrations

- exchanging information verbally

- challenging their peers with such word pattern puzzles as: "What's my rule: *toast, telephone, number, ribbon, no, open?*" (Answer: each successive word starts with the final sound of the preceding word. This is an extension of the previously discussed phonemic segmentation.)

- telling jokes (Books with such titles as *The World's Worst Monster Jokes* are sure-fire hits.)

- trying to make definitions (Their attempts are apt to refer to function: scissors are things to cut with. The ability to define by category and saliency comes later. These are the baby steps.)

- bring the mechanics of handwriting close to an automatic level. (This is particularly true in schools that abandon the arcane, unnecessary custom of teaching printing or manuscript in K and 1, introducing cursive in mid-2nd grade but not letting students use it, then requiring cursive one magical day in 3rd grade. This layering of manual systems is unproductive. Students should learn one system—my choice is manuscript or D'Nealian—and then learn correct keyboard fingering in 4th or 5th grades, and have the option to learn cursive, if they would like to, as an extra or a club activity. Kids should practice and reinforce their manual skills, bringing them to such automaticity that no attentional energy is drained from thinking or creating by manual requirements and memory of how a letter is formed or where it should sit on the line.)

With these elements in mind, we can easily see which kids are on target, which are in need of a boost, and which are floundering. It goes without saying that children who have been "baby-sat" and "massaged," rather than really taught, will be behind. One peril of the "Whole Language Or Bust—Absorption Will Take Care Of Everything—Direct Instruction Is Repressive" point of view is that it has seeped into teacher training programs. As a result, we are seeing populations of teachers who haven't been taught the structure of language themselves and therefore cannot impart it to students.

Metacognition in second grade: what are we looking for, why does it matter, how do we assess?

Second graders are ready to solidify their ideas of time. They can and should:

- know the days of the week, the months of the year, and the four seasons in order

- be able to tell time from the face of an analog clock as well as a digital one

- learn to monitor elapsing time: in ten minutes, after an hour, tomorrow, etc.

- be able to use such words as *first, next, finally, later, after,* and *before* in governing their own behavior and planning their work and play

- be able to understand and use verb tenses accurately, and keep a personal time line in mind.

Time is an invisible concept, accessible only through language. It is vital to planning, thinking, and remembering. Many of today's children, accustomed as they are to living in the moment, don't solidify this foundation and thus find themselves in later years confused, late, or not having left enough time to accomplish what needs to be done.

Second graders are also ready to begin thinking about their reading in terms of the 6 *wh* words: *who, what, when, where, why,* and *how.* These form an organizational grid on which to sort, file, and retrieve information, thereby making it available for the convergence zones mentioned earlier and for use in working memory.

Moving from simple counting, second graders are ready to expand the foundations of mathematical thinking (hopefully) established earlier. They thrive on challenges such as "How many ways can we think of to build the number 20?" They may well answer 10+10, 23 -3, 5+5+5+5, 15+10-5, etc.

Playing with numbers at an early age goes a long way toward preventing math anxiety or phobia.

Red flags

The kid who has trouble mapping speech sounds onto print is sending a warning. When the child writes words that are only similar-sounding first cousins to the intended words, the child is showing difficulty with sound recognition in the *receptive* system, distortions in the *expressive* system, and skewed concepts in *metacognition.*

Here is an example which enfolds all three kinds of concerns in one package. This is a story written by a second grade boy who was trying to write about what might happen if Amelia Bedelia played hockey. This is a transcription of his actual spelling; a translation follows.

Amelia Bedelia play hockey
Amelia Bedelia lose to play hockey and on the street Amelia Bedelia sol a sine in sed Hockey team. cum pla. Amelia Bedelia was icsided. and trid aut. sow that night Amelia Bedelia played hockey but she got mixed up when she was off sides she siad howcan I take off the sides and wend she got a peneldey she said bo I have to go to Jail or bo I havet to pay a fine and wen the coche said check that go and she said I mush have chech bord to check the go. Amelia Bedelia shot from the blue line and in whend past the player and the goley and even went theo the net and scord!! but not better than me.

Translation:

Amelia Bedelia Played Hockey
Amelia Bedelia loves to play hockey and on the street
Amelia Bedelia saw a sign. It said Hockey Team: come play.
Amelia Bedelia was excited and tried out. So that night
Amelia Bedelia played hockey but she got mixed up when she
was off sides. She said, "How can I take off the sides?" and
when she got a penalty she said "Do I have to go to jail or do
I have to pay a fine?" And when the coach said "Check that
goal" and she said "I must have a check board to check the
goal." Amelia Bedelia shot from the blue line and in (it) went
past the player and the goalie and even went through the net
and scored!! but not better than me!

Lose/loves, sol/saw, bo/do, go/goal, play/played are illustra-
tive of the errors in perception in the *receptive* domain (*sol/
saw* or *lose/loves*), the *expressive* domain (*bo/do*), and the
metacognitive area (*play/played*). These perceptual confusions,
perhaps symptoms of disability or dyslexia, caused the child's
errors in encoding that rob the story of its sense.

Perhaps this is an appropriate place to distinguish between perceptually prompted errors and what is called *invented*
or *natural* spelling. In some schools, students are encouraged
to just write down the sounds they think might make the
word they are trying to write. Accuracy is not the goal, and,
in fact, some teachers say that emphasis on accuracy
squelches creativity. While this is true to a degree, children
enjoy knowing the correct way to write a word and are proud

to write what others can read. It is very easy to teach correct spelling patterns as part of teaching sound/symbol correspondence, while also letting the child take a flyer on unfamiliar words. Children need *both* approaches. They are not incompatible.

The best way to assess *metacognition* is to be aware of its cloaks, on the lookout for daggers, and alert to its disappearance.

Suggested activities

Receptive language

1. The game of I Spy With My Little Eye fosters and requires careful listening, not to mention thinking. "It" spots an object in plain sight and says, "I Spy With My Little Eye something red." Classmates try to discover the object by asking yes or no questions. (For example, the old classic from What's My Line—"Is it bigger than a breadbox?" Substitute the term *microwave oven* for today's listeners.) The possibilities narrow down through process of elimination. If "It" has said that the object is not bigger than a breadbox or a microwave, it would be foolish to guess that the object is the red door to the supplies closet. Children who struggle with this game should learn to repeat the questions and answers to themselves, adding a bit of interpretation. This helps lodge the information more securely in their minds: "No, it's not *bigger* than a breadbox...so it's *smaller* than a breadbox."

2. Here comes read-aloud poetry again. This time, the teacher chooses a poem, reads it aloud while students close their eyes and visualize the images the author is creating. Then, they open their eyes and write about the most vivid image. The progression from kindergarten has been first to hear and draw, then hear and say, and now hear and write.

3. The teacher says a word while the children listen and count the number of syllables—or chunks—they hear. Then, they hold up a corresponding number of fingers. Teachers should start with one-, two-, and three-syllable words. Once children can discriminate accurately in this group, the teacher can move quickly to two-, three-, four-, five-, or six-syllable words.

These activities help children hone the precision of their language intake.

Expressive language

1. By second grade, children whose explanatory skills are marginal need to practice them. Here's a way. The teacher displays a collection of puppets and asks each child to pick two. Then, the child plays a game of Why And Why Not, with puppets taking different points of view. For example, the teacher might say "Today's discussion revolves around whether chocolate ice cream is a good breakfast. Let one puppet be in favor and the other puppet against. The ground rule is that each puppet must have a minimum of three specific reasons, such as: chocolate has both fat and sugar and isn't that good for you, or kids who can have chocolate ice

cream for breakfast won't come to school hungry." Other topics might include the pros and cons of TV, or the existence or nonexistence of extraterrestrial life. As with all the suggestions in this book, the only limitation is the teacher's imagination.

2. In Hear And Extend, the teacher reads a story aloud. Then, each child picks one character (human or animal) and makes that character the central figure in a new story that the child will tell or write.

3. The teacher can ask the children to help build a collection of compound words. The teacher writes each word on some specially shaped, pre-cut piece of paper. For example, one teacher used paper in the shape of a foot. She wrote the children's compound words on foot paper and stuck them on the wall of the classroom—continuing out into the hall and all the way to the lunch room.

These activities, while they will not solve serious expressive language problems, will help children feel fluent and comfortable producing their ideas.

Metacognition

1. Here comes the Feely Bag yet another time. In this instance and at this level, start with an empty bag. Ask one child to find two objects in the room that share a tangible attribute (hard, bendy, slippery, sharp) and put them in the Feely Bag. The next child reaches in, feels around, and must

say the attribute the two objects share. For example, "I feel a block and a pencil. They are both hard."

2. Here are some ways to lock in the concept of time. Because so many children have had digital watches all their lives and can read the numbers on the LED screen, they create the illusion that they understand time. Teachers need to have an analog (round face with hands) clock on display in their classrooms and show students how to use it. In addition, they need to have a big calendar on display, and at the end of each school day one child should draw a little rebus of something which happened to the group that day (Mary had a birthday, Josh threw up, it rained). When a week or so has gone by, the calendar will provide a time line of the group's activities, and the teacher can ask, "How many birthdays have we had this week?" or "How many days did we not have rain?" Time and calendars become meaningful as children attach their own experiences and own language to the empty squares. Teachers can also color code activities on the calendar: "On Mondays, we have music, I'll put a blue star on each Monday," etc. (Teachers interested in further information about helping students really understand and chart the nature of time should consult the how-to section on time in Chapter 10 of my book *"Words Fail Me!"*—see the resource section—which provides a carefully sequenced set of activities.)

3. Ask each child to put a set of magnetic letters in alphabetical order (excellent preparation for later use of telephone books, dictionaries, and stadium seating). Then, ask each

child to construct a nonsense word and give it a meaning. Perhaps it will be something to eat, a new sport, a vehicle for transportation. Finally, the child should illustrate and label it.

These activities are designed to practice the fine art of comparison, to give concrete form to the abstraction of time, and to open opportunities for the exercise of imagination.

Case study

Adam and Francine entered second grade with their reputations preceding them: "Francine is the bright one, she's really something. She'll need enrichment and all kinds of extra opportunities for expansion. Poor Adam. It must be hard to have such a bright twin sister and be so much slower."

Francine's handwriting was precise and even rather elegant. Sometimes, she decorated her capital letters, making her paper look like a manuscript annotated by a medieval monk. Her spelling was mirror-image perfect. She continued to be very quick with her arithmetic combinations and always wrote her sums in tidy columns and rows. She enjoyed keeping the calendar on the classroom wall and was particularly proud to count out the cookies for snack. She also liked helping the teacher take attendance and ferrying the information to the school office. But, strangely, she didn't enjoy games of "How many ways could we think of to make the number 20?" And she seemed physically uncomfortable if her teacher said, "Let's think of several different ways of telling that the kitten in the story was sad."

Adam's handwriting continued to sprawl. When he got "icsided" (excited) about the content of something he was writing, he would omit letters, words, or sometimes even whole phrases. He couldn't proofread his own work, because what he had intended to say was so vivid and immediate that he couldn't see what was missing on the paper. His reading was either slow and methodical or rushed and inaccurate. He couldn't seem to hit a rhythmic stride. In arithmetic, he sometimes reversed his numerals; he covered his papers with pictures of triangles, parallelograms, and other geometric shapes; and his rote memory was unreliable. He continued to be a physically active child who could stay at a desk for twenty to thirty minutes but then had to walk off all that thinking.

Hmmmm.

CHAPTER FIVE

Third Grade Language Assessment: What, Why, How

The child whose language development is robust through third grade acquires the intellectual equipment to make solid progress throughout the remaining years of school. The child whose language is spongy, weak, faltering, poorly nourished, moth-eaten, paltry, or unexercised is headed for academic trouble all the rest of the way. The importance of this year's developments cannot be overstated.

Neurologist Richard Masland explains that early reading is a form of pattern recognition, relying heavily on the brain's right hemisphere. Later, real, deep reading is a form of language recognition, drawing on the brain's own capacity for language, which in most right-handed people is located in the left hemisphere. The shift occurs at third grade.

Neurologist and psychiatrist Milton Horowitz points out that this is also the age for dramatic brain mass increase and the time when the corpus callosum thickens its coat of myelin, allowing messages to flash back and forth between the two hemispheres in a way not possible before.

Third grade is a year of major changes in *receptive* language, *expressive* language, and *metacognition*. Third graders negotiate their social situations verbally: joking, wheedling, cajoling. In the classroom, they move from *learning to read* to *reading to learn*. Word problems appear in arithmetic. The child who is unclear about the meaning of the word *each* will stumble over "Brian, Ted, John, and Fred each had a pack of gum. Each pack held five pieces. How many pieces were there altogether?" Although arithmetically the kid might be able to add 5+5+5+5 and produce the answer 20, the "*each*-misser" may add four boys to five pieces of gum and proudly say, "Nine."

Frequently, parents think that once a child has learned to talk, language is all set. Wrong. Also, teachers with many students, little time, and thickets of bureaucracy and paperwork may not have learned about the importance of language development at this particular level. If they have, they may not know how to interpret or assess their students' prowess, and are not sure what to do for those who need shoring up. (For a detailed profile of individual students and the whole class, as well as specific suggestions for help, readers may want to use my Third and Fourth Grade Language Screening—test materials and a manual for administration, scoring, interpretation, and assistance. See the resource section for details.)

In any event, following the organization that is familiar by now, we will look at *receptive* language, *expressive* language, *metacognition*, as well as red flags and a case study.

Receptive language in third grade: what are we looking for, why does it matter, how do we assess?

Third graders read for information as well as for the delights of fiction. Classically, this is the year to read about the explorers, perhaps choosing one to study and report on in detail.

We need to probe third graders' silent—not just oral—reading. Just because a kid looks comfortable in a chair doesn't mean that meaning is soaking through the reading. As we watch children read silently, we need to note whether they:

• appear to be comfortable

• move their eyes smoothly across the lines of print or jolt forward, stop, re-track, and surge ahead again

• sub-vocalize either silently or audibly (Kids who sub-vocalize are the ones who in later years go to the library and study quietly for several hours, emerging with a sore throat.)

• proceed at roughly the same pace as their peers

• look worried or try to show off by being fast.

We also need to hear each child read aloud, noting:

• accuracy

• rhythm

• ease or strain of voice

• recognition of sight words

• ability to decode

• familiarity with vocabulary

• sense of anticipation: knowing via linguistic hunch what words the writer is surely going to use next.

Then, we need to assess their comprehension. A good way is to prepare and ask two questions in each of the five following categories:

• main idea

• inference

• vocabulary

• fact retrieval

• sequence.

We must notice whether each child's performance and comprehension are stronger in oral or silent reading, and then share this information with the student: "Sam, when you come to a piece of reading that's really important, do yourself a favor and read it out loud. Your memory and thinking seem much stronger for passages you have heard in your own voice." Or "Melanie, it seems that when you read out loud, the sound of your voice or the effort to speak it all out distracts you from the content of what you're meant to focus on. Your memory and thinking are much stronger for passages you read silently." Encourage kids to use such information to help themselves.

Third graders should also be able to:

- carry out a three- to four-part set of directions or instructions

- understand and make puns

- dish out playground lingo quickly and gleefully

- understand figures of speech and proverbs.

Expressive language in third grade: what are we looking for, why does it matter, how do we assess?

Third graders' *expressive* language skills show best through the things they think are funny:

- puns

- tongue twisters

- Spoonerisms *(the queer old dean /the dear old queen)*

- Pig Latin *(the eer-quay old-ay ean-day/the ear-day old-day een-quay).*

Obviously, these slices of humor are phonemic segmentation all grown up. Kids who cannot engage in this appealing silliness are indicating that they are in trouble.

We also see the level of their language development through their ability to:

- make a definition, moving from something concrete/visible to something more abstract: *finger, young* (Making a definition requires an overview as well as a microscope.)

- be storytellers in the classic ceremonial mode of sitting at a table or on a stool, having a lantern or other amulet to signify the start of a performance, and telling a rehearsed tale. (Telling a story requires vocabulary, rhythm, cadence, and "voice.")

For a general assessment of third graders' expressive language skills, entice them into the above domains through a book, conversation, or opportunity. Notice where they stumble and where they shine. Teach accordingly.

Metacognition in third grade: what are we looking for, why does it matter, how do we assess?

As third graders reflect on their own thinking and talk about their own language *in* their own language, we see them:

- moving from the concrete to the figurative

- developing thick bundles of association with which they support and fatten their working memory, semantic memory, remote memory, and episodic memory powers

- beginning to think in analogy—not simply answering an analogy question such as hot:cold :: wet:?, but really thinking analogously. ("The way the king and the soldiers managed the end of the battle was like the way Lewis and Clark coped with the cold mud.")

To assess third graders' skills in this area, listen to their spontaneous and rehearsed/prepared language, with an ear to their ease or difficulty with such figurative constructions as simile and metaphor. Chart which kinds of memory they draw from accurately, and which present problems. Offer some analogy problems for them to answer. Errors or difficulty in any of these deserve attention and help.

71

Red flags

The student who is stuck at a concrete level and doesn't move into abstract or figurative language is headed for trouble. Here are two examples.

Luis took home his spelling lists to study for the weekly Wednesday test. On the list were days of the week and, in preparation for a project, the terminology of baseball. The teacher said, "Study Monday and Tuesday." Luis studied the words *Monday* and *Tuesday* and didn't know what had gone wrong.

Agatha listened to the poem the teacher read aloud. The children had been asked to construct mental imagery for what they were hearing. The poem, "The Whole Duty of Berkshire Brooks" by Grace Conkling, contains the phrases:

"...to build the trout a crystal stair
to comb the hillside's thick green hair..."

Agatha said, "That's dumb. I don't get it. Fish can't walk."

Suggested activities

Receptive language

1. Play Twenty Questions. This is a notch higher and harder than I Spy With My Little Eye, cited in the previous chapter. As a review of the rules, "It" selects something either animal, vegetable, or mineral that must be in the room. The group tries to figure out what it is by asking yes or no questions, but only twenty are allowed. Strong players quickly

figure out that large-scale, process-of-elimination questions are strategic, while single shots are a waste early on: "Is it in the front half of the room?" vs. "Is it the wastebasket?"

2. Another way to use read-aloud poetry is for the teacher to read a poem aloud while the students have their eyes closed. When the poem is over, each child thinks of something the poem reminds him or her of. The teacher is looking for association, not repetition.

3. A wise teacher will give third graders ample opportunities to play with puns—meat and drink to this age. Children especially enjoy writing and illustrating their own books of puns. The teacher should provide ample preparation by illustrating the nature of a pun, showing examples of how single words can have multiple meanings, and collecting from the group pairs of words which have the same sound but different meanings: *steel/steal, maid/made,* etc.

Expressive language

1. Use Puppet Theater in a more complicated way at this level. The teacher provides a collection of puppets. Each child chooses one. The teacher also writes some simple actions on index cards (brush your teeth, put on your pajamas, wash the dishes, look up a word in the dictionary, etc.) Taking turns, each child picks a card and a partner. The puppet has to explain in detail to the partner how to do the task, and the partner must pantomime each step the puppet says. This is harder than it sounds and is great practice for giving expla-

nations. (Actually, some adults could use a little polishing in this domain.)

2. With the group and with individual children, collect and illustrate figures of speech, drawing both the literal image and interpretive meaning. For example, "hard-hearted" could be drawn as a heart made of rock and then as a person unmoved in pitiable circumstances.

3. Without saying a title, the teacher reads a brief story to the group. After a discussion about the story, each child is asked to create a title. This requires memory and chunking of ideas, followed by the ability to summarize—a skill vital for strong expressive language.

Metacognition

1. Enter the Feely Bag one more time. At this level, ask one student to select from the room—or from his or her personal belongings—two objects with opposite attributes. Hide them in the empty Feely Bag and choose another student to feel around, figure out what's there, and explain why they are opposite. For example, a tissue and a comb: soft and hard.

2. Collect from the group a list of those words that organize behavior in the language of time: *unless, if, until, whenever, always, never, sometimes, later, after, before*, etc. Write the words on Post-it notes and stick them in a line around the wall of the room. Ask each child to choose one of the words and use it in a sentence. Then, pick the Post-it note from the

wall and attach it to the paper with the sentence. Pass that paper to the next child, asking that child to add a new sentence using the word, etc.

3. Another use of the Feely Bag is to fill it full of familiar objects, then ask each child to select an object, display it to the group, and describe it with a simile: "This paper clip is as silvery as the smile of a kid wearing braces." Try to avoid the cliches.

These activities encourage the intertwining of language, thought, and experience.

Case history

As Adam and Francine progressed through third grade, things began to change. Francine did well on comprehension exercises involving factual recall or rote memory, but she didn't catch on to inference. She understood what was in black and white, but not what was between the lines. She had trouble identifying the main idea because she didn't enjoy sorting or thinking hierarchically. She had trouble with sequence questions if they involved any flashbacks or fast-forwards. She memorized her multiplication tables and won class rounds of Around The World, but she stumbled badly over word problems. Her handwriting remained lovely, but her stories were concrete-bound, and she didn't catch on to the jokes in *The King Who Rained.*

As she felt herself slipping academically, she held on too tightly to her friends, fearing that they, too, might slip away.

They felt tethered and wanted to branch out. Quarrels ensued, along with hurt feelings and unkind humor. Third grade girls have Olympic isolation skills which they turned on Francine. She didn't know what she had done wrong, what was happening, or how to become reconnected. For solace, her parents gave her a guinea pig, which delighted her and provided a perfect outlet for her emotional warmth.

Adam's pencil finally submitted to the will of his energetic mind. The teacher excused him from having to learn cursive, and he stayed with his own idiosyncratic form of printing. He was mesmerized by the explorers, read everything he could lay his hands on about Lewis and Clark, and made six shoebox dioramas depicting their adventures. He also wrote his own book, *Disgusting Jokes for Third Graders*. With his arithmetic facts finally mastered, he was intrigued with the practical application of word problems, saying, "Oh, now I get what math is for!" He continued to be physically energetic and gained a solid place in the group, not only for his general kindness and decency, but because he was a strong soccer player.

What's next for these two?

CHAPTER SIX

Fourth Grade Language Assessment: What, Why, How

The following comments apply to fourth grade and beyond. Many of today's students have not solidified the skills
described below or those of earlier levels. Unless they fill in
the holes, they will struggle to make sense of school, work,
and life.

As I am writing this, a master carpenter is working his
magic on a needy corner of our house. I studied his tool belt
this morning, finding there: hammer, chisels, nails and nail
set, razor knife, pencil, combination square, and tape measure. These parallel the language tools the ready fourth grader
will have collected over the years. The hammer of language
represents power and joining. Verbal nails hold ideas and
concepts together. Metaphoric razor knives are for cutting
and scoring the sheetrock of information, sharpening the
pencils of expression, and for intricate precision. The combination square helps keep ideas in proper alignment, and the
tape measure speaks for itself. In *receptive* language, *expressive*

language, and *metacognition*, the fourth grader has been hanging his equipment through the loops of the language tool belt which will help him master the jobs at hand.

Receptive language in fourth grade: what are we looking for, why does it matter, how do we assess?

Having accumulated the *receptive* tools mentioned in the previous sections, the fourth grader—or an older student—incorporates earlier levels in the never-ending spiral of language development. Students:

- organize their intake of listening and reading according to the 6 *wh* words: *who, what, when, where, why, how*

- enjoy chanting the silly, beautiful, or ghostly poetry they learned by heart in the past, being ready now to add bits of Wordsworth, Shakespeare, or T.S. Eliot (Some may still need Shel Silverstein, but they should begin to taste more sophisticated fare.)

- still need to hear stories, poems, and essays read aloud. (No student is ever too old for this, and yet, in a deprivation that is intended to mark rites of passage to adulthood, we often stop reading aloud to kids this age. "They already know how to read," "They should practice themselves," or "We don't have time—there's too much to cover.")

Most of all, in normal development, the language process and structure is so solid that kids this age readily recognize language patterns even in a nonsense passage. At the 1997 International Conference of the British Dyslexia Association, Dr. Gavin Reid of the University of Edinburgh distributed the example below, entitled *Mosanda*, to the many adults assembled in his session.

He pointed out that deep familiarity with language structures—such as nouns, proper nouns, verbs, verb tense endings (*s, ing,* or *ed*), adjectives, adverbs, and word position in declarative sentences and questions—allows people to identify these linguistic elements even in a nonsense piece.

Then, he asked the group to "read" *Mosanda*. At first, people squirmed, wriggled, scratched their heads, furrowed their brows, and looked like kids in a classroom being given a test that's too hard. But then lights came on, and so did laughter. Once readers let their language recognition guide them, the way was easy.

As the old commercial goes, "try it...you'll like it".

Mosanda
Mosanda is an amient grot with many flits. It slanks from gorite, an ild which pargs like lange. Mosanda slickles several other parances, which farkers expart by tarking the gorite and larping it in shranker-clarsped frobs. The parances glark a

79

chark which is langed with shwoters, tranking a blorp. This blorp is garped through several other terrosces, finally trasting a tragety, flickant, brankle. The mosanda is expargunt, grinkling, and borigen. It is exacerated from the boridge by means of floracity.

Five Questions

1. What is mosanda? Draw it.

2. What does mosanda slank from?

3. How do farkers expart the parances from the gorite?

4. What does the blorp finally trast?

5. How is the mosanda exacerated from the boridge?

Here's a sample of one fourth grade student's translation.

Miranda

Miranda is a lively creature with many wings. It hides from lethal-lizard, a predator which pounces like cats. Miranda mates with several other species, which insures survival by outnumbering the lethal-lizard, and paralyzing it in bark-sharpened talons. The other species navigate a forest which is hung with mosses, hiding a unicorn. This unicorn is glimpsed through several other camouflages, finally showing a glittery, smooth hide. The miranda is unendangered, vegetarian, and tameable. It is protected from the elements by means of waterproofing.

How do we know that *mosanda* is a noun? By its place in the sentence. How do we know it is a not a proper noun? It is only capitalized at the beginning of the sentence. How do we know that *slank* is a verb? By its position in the sentence and the addition of *s*. How do we know that *farkers* is a plural noun? By its position in the sentence and the addition of *s* to indicate plural. How do we know that *blorp* and *trast* are, respectively, a noun and a verb? By their positions in the sentence. How do we know that *exacerated* is a passive construction? By the presence of *how is the*, followed by a verb ending in *ed*. How do we know that *floracity* is a process or condition? By its ending, *ity*.

Is there a correct translation of *Mosanda*? Of course not. Like the game of Mad Libs, the "reader" can use any nouns, verbs, or adjectives that conform to the language patterns laid out in the piece.

Children who catch on to the patterns and clues in this passage are showing a fully developed sense of morphology, syntax, and deep structure, which allow them intuitive recognition of author's intent when they set about actual vs. nonsense reading. Use this example to assess where individual students are. Ask some of the most verbally facile kids to invent some similar passages and questions. Can they follow the structural rules when they compose as well as when they interpret?

Expressive language in fourth grade: what are we looking for, why does it matter, how do we assess?

By fourth grade, students are expected to:

- organize their spoken output, staying on the subject, using contrasting expressions such as "on the other hand" or "but," being able to keep a plot or historical events in sequence, and using the tools of strong verbs and interesting adjectives to flavor their offerings

- organize their written output, using classical outlining, mind mapping, or the color/shape method described in *Clear & Lively Writing* and *Learning Styles*, in which they learn to attach a color value to each of the 6 *wh* words and conform their writing to a triangle, an upside down triangle, a square, a diamond, or an hour glass (In spite of the prevalence of computers and printers, students this age should develop a manual writing system in order to have what the neurologists call "kinetic melody"—an easy, harmonious flow between mind and hand.)

- convert concepts they are learning in math into prose (Some students have simply learned the formulaic rituals of, let's say, long division.

They know when to move from right to left or left to right, when to drop down, and when to zoom back up, but they don't know why. The best math teaching requires them to learn long division and at each step to explain what they are doing and why in clear English sentences. Math, after all, is a language and a symbol system, just as words and sentences are. Students with deep understanding can translate back and forth.)

- summarize what they are learning or have learned. (To summarize, one must have a global understanding of the concept and a firm grasp on its components. Then, one must be able to select the salient features and describe them concisely, hewing closely to the details but not being "Gullivered" by them. The Princeton Minute, so called because it was written up in a Princeton University publication, asks teachers to take a few minutes at the end of every class session and ask students to write the answers to:

What did I learn in this class?

What am I confused/uncertain about?

What would I like to learn more about?

Students who use the Princeton minute regularly show improved memory, stronger focus, and richer convergence zones. Regular practice in summarizing sharpens the language skills of comprehension, filing, storage, and retrieval throughout life.)

Metacognition in fourth grade: what are we looking for, why does it matter, how do we assess?

Fourth graders are ready to think about what they have been thinking about:

- by harvesting information and then by learning to ask the winnowing question— eliminating extraneous information or putting it aside for later use

- by harnessing the power of their own Executive Function, which neurologist Martha Denckla describes as being comprised of four abilities in the acronym of the Egyptian deity ISIS:

Initiate thought or action

Sustain thought or action

Inhibit distractions from without or within

Shift focus or attention to a new direction

- by pre-structuring their investigations and thinking, using five Key Questions:

What do I already know?

What do I need to find out?

Where will I find the information I need?

How will I collate, store, and use this information?

What is my final goal?

- by exercising their newly emergent capacity for dealing with ambiguity—holding two opposing ideas in their heads simultaneously and shuttling between them.

Here's an exercise adapted from a talk I heard given by Joseph Procacino, a professor at Georgetown University. He said "*Never say No.*' Does that mean acquiescing to every request? By no means, but try to find a light way of giving an unmistakable message. For example, if a teenage daughter says she would like to invite a boy she met at camp to come for the weekend and wants to know if he can sleep in her room, the answer could be, 'Of course, as long as there are two full moons in the sky on the same night.'"

Fourth graders are newly able to understand and invent examples of what I call Procacino's Ambiguity, and they like to use the term. It sounds very hard and adult. They might ask and answer such questions as: "May I eat this blueberry pie before dinner?" "May I take all the change off the top of

Dad's bureau?" "May I auction off my little brother?" Incidentally, Procacino's Ambiguity is an ideal moment to teach the *can I/may I* distinction.

Red flags

Danger signals at this level (and beyond) include:

- inaccurate reading and, to a lesser extent, spelling

- arrhythmia in speaking or handwriting

- difficulty with word retrieval, known clinically as *dysnomia*, showing in speech as consistent use of time buyers and fillers such as "um..."

- class clown behavior—a classic camouflage for insufficiently developed language

- avoidance of written work: "How long does it have to be?" "The dog ate my homework." "I left it on the desk." "I love the science experiments, but I hate keeping the notebook." "I don't know." "I don't care." (These are representative early indicators of Developmental Output Failure Syndrome. This dislike of written work grows into reluctance to share ideas on paper or in class, and comes into full flower as global avoidance of intellectual engagement, usually around 8th grade. Once established, it is very difficult to reverse. It either takes root or doesn't, depending on the student's ease or discomfort with written output at fourth grade.)

Suggested activities

Receptive language

1. Play the game of Twenty Questions, delineated in the activities section of the previous chapter. But students at this level are ready for higher levels of abstraction. Whatever "It" decides on need not be visible but could be a character from history, a distant object such as the moon, or a type of appliance such as a television, microwave oven, or CD player. As in the earlier levels, careful listening and cataloguing of the answers to the questions are necessary.

2. As a further extension of earlier suggestions involving read-aloud poetry, after the students have listened to the poem and seen it on the screens of their minds, ask each one to select one image and use it in constructing a new poem.

3. Ask each child to select a poem to learn by heart and to recite to the group. It can be one of the read-alouds or a completely different one. Knowing a poem by heart is a nourishment to the heart, mind, and soul, and furthermore provides relief from boredom, discomfort, or anxiety—as when stuck in a traffic jam, undergoing labor pains, enduring insomnia.

These activities rehearse listening skills and drench kids in the lyricism of poetry.

Expressive language

1. The teacher presents a dilemma to the class. An example might be: "The school budget for this year has been set. There are enough funds to build three new classrooms *or* a science lab. Which are you in favor of, and why?" Ask each child to pick one side of the issue and write a highly persuasive plea for that cause.

2. Then, ask each child to take the opposite side and write an equally persuasive plea.

3. Then, ask each child to list three factors most likely to influence his or her personal decision, three factors most likely to sway the opposition, and the three factors the local newspaper would be likely to highlight in an editorial.

These activities help kids move back and forth between and among points of view—a symptom of newly developed language skills—and practice reinforcing new growth.

Metacognition

1. The teacher should create extra opportunities for students to work with the five Key Questions listed in an earlier section of this chapter:

What do I already know?

What do I need to find out?

Where will I find the information I need?

How will I collate, store, and use this information?

What is my final goal?

Once these are laid out, the teacher should give students ample practice in remembering and applying these vital organizational guidelines.

2. Here comes the Feely Bag for yet another, higher level. The teacher should collect three items each from five categories, such as general school supplies, personal grooming, items used in writing, things to eat, household items. List the categories, but not the individual items, for the students. Then, ask each, in turn, to come up, feel in the bag, and pick three items which belong in the same category.

3. Using alphabetical order, brainstorm with the group a genre of literature for each letter. For example, *a*=autobiography, *b*=brainteasers, *c*=comedy, *d*=drama, etc. This exercise in and of itself helps students catalogue and categorize distinctions they understand intuitively but may not have articulated. With this collection posted on the wall, the teacher can then show that since there are 26 letters in the alphabet and roughly 26 weeks in the school year, by careful choice in what's to be read aloud, the group can probably sample each category or genre.

These activities use language to extend the boundaries of thought.

Case study

Because Adam's and Francine's parents and teachers were perplexed by the twins' evolving patterns of strengths and weaknesses, they decided a full scale psycho-educational evaluation was in order. Both children scored a Full Scale I.Q. of 118.

How could children whose patterns and performance are so different come up with the same number? An I.Q. score is simply a composite, not even an average. The final number is derived from scores on subtests in both *verbal* and *performance* categories. Thus, the full scale number gives no indication of highs and lows within the subtests.

In this instance, Francine showed excellent attention to visual detail and lightning-quick facility with coding (learning new geometric symbols and reproducing them rapidly and accurately in the small slots provided in the test booklet), all while under the gun of the stopwatch. Her ability to understand and describe similarities and differences, however, was well below other children her age. Her mechanics were high and her reasoning low.

Adam was just the opposite. His coding score was only 7, compared to a national norm of 10 and a possible range of 1 to 19. His block design score, indicating three-dimensional reasoning, was 19—the highest you can go. In conceptualization, he was way out ahead, but in mechanics he was weaker than most children his age on a national scale.

Truly, these non-identical twins created an academic yin and yang. But what do all these scores and patterns mean?

Children who start out with meticulous facility are often mistakenly considered outstanding thinkers. Some of them may be, but there is no guarantee. Many boys who start out with trouble in the mechanical and symbolic areas will start to soar at around third grade, if they have had systematic training using multi-sensory methods and materials in the preceding years. To minimize or withhold such teaching is to compromise what may be outstanding intelligence, and create a perpetual need for catch-up in someone whose energies should be directed to contributions to both the juvenile and adult worlds.

Adam and Francine each have strong, valuable contributions to make to their and our worlds. Their use of language differs: Francine uses language for registering, recording, and remembering, while Adam uses language for thinking and inventing. The world needs both skills and must honor differences accordingly.

Language assessment allows adults to recognize children's innate and individual language patterns, to strengthen those in need, to reinforce those which are robust, and to enjoy—with children and one another—the human miracle of language.

CONCLUSION

The braid of language is formed by the three strands of *receptive* language, *expressive* language, and *metacognition*. The fatter each strand and the nimbler the fingers of the braider, the lovelier, shinier, and stronger the braid will be.

It is the job and privilege of concerned adults to understand the importance of these three components, to notice their presence or absense intuitively, and to measure what's going in, what's rumbling around inside, and what's coming out, using our trusty language yardstick.

RESOURCE SECTION

Three Organizations

Modern Learning Press, Box 167, Rosemont, NJ 08556 (1-800-627-5867). This excellent publishing house offers a wide variety of wholly reliable, exciting materials for educators and parents. They are a welcome resource.

Educators Publishing Service, 31 Smith Place, Cambridge, MA 02138. This publisher offers multi-sensory and organizational materials, originally designed for dyslexics, which work magnificently in regular classrooms. The descriptions and age/grade levels in their catalogues are scrupulously fair.

The Orton Dyslexia Society, Chester Building, Suite 382, 8600 LaSalle Rd., Baltimore, MD 21204-6020. This organization, now called The International Dyslexia Association, brings together physicians, researchers, educators, and parents, offering excellent publications and conferences open to any interested participant.

General Bibliography

Priscilla Vail's books

(Available from Modern Learning Press—see previous page.)

About Dyslexia: Unraveling the Myth. Rosemont, NJ: Modern Learning Press, 1990.

Clear & Lively Writing: Language Games and Activities for Everyone. New York: Walker & Co., 1981.

Common Ground: Whole Language and Phonics Working Together. Rosemont, NJ: Modern Learning Press, 1991.

Emotion: The On/Off Switch for Learning. Rosemont, NJ: Modern Learning Press, 1994.

Gifted, Precocious, or Just Plain Smart. Rosemont, NJ: Modern Learning Press, 1987.

Learning Styles: Food for Thought and 130 Practical Tips. Rosemont, NJ: Modern Learning Press, 1992.

Smart Kids With School Problems: Things to Know and Ways to Help. New York: NAL Plume Paperback, 1989.

The World of the Gifted Child. New York: Walker & Co., 1979 (currently between printings, available through libraries).

Third/Fourth Grade Language Screening. Rosemont, NJ: Modern Learning Press, 1998.

"Words Fail Me!"—How Language Works and What Happens When It Doesn't. Rosemont, NJ: Modern Learning Press, 1996.

Other Authors and Titles

Erikson, Erik. *Childhood & Society.* New York: W.W. Norton, 1950.

Fraiberg, Selma. *The Magic Years.* New York: Charles Scribner's Sons, 1959.

Galaburda, Albert. *From Reading to Neurons.* Cambridge, MA: MIT Press, 1989.

Gardner, Howard. *Frames of Mind: the Theory of Multiple Intelligences.* New York: Basic Books, 1984.

Hallowell, Edward M., and Thompson, Michael G. *Finding the Heart of the Child.* Braintree, MA: Association of Independent Schools of Massachusetts, 1993.

Hallowell, Edward M., and Ratey, John J. *Driven to Distraction: Attention Deficit Disorder in Children and Adults.* New York: Pantheon Books, 1994.

Healy, Jane M. *Your Child's Growing Mind.* New York: Doubleday, 1987.

Healy, Jane M. *Endangered Minds.* New York: Doubleday, 1989.

Henry, Marcia. *Words.* Los Gatos, CA: Lex Press.

deHirsch, Katrina. *Language and the Developing Child.* Baltimore: the Orton Dyslexia Society, Monograph #4, 1984.

Levine, Mel. *Keeping a Head in School.* Cambridge, MA: Educator's Publishing Service, 1990.

Luria, A. *The Mind of a Mnemonist.* Cambridge, MA: Harvard University Press, 1968.

Pinker, Steven. *The Language Instinct.* New York: William Morrow, 1994.

Pinker, Steven. *How the Mind Works.* New York: W.W. Norton and Company, 1997.

Rawson, Margaret. *The Many Faces of Dyslexia.* Baltimore: Orton Dyslexia Society, 1989.

Restak, Richard. *The Brain Has a Mind of Its Own.* New York: Crown, 1991.

Rosner, Jerome. *Helping Children Overcome Learning Difficulties.* New York: Walker & Co., 1980.

Seligman, Martin E.P. *The Optimistic Child.* New York: Knopf, 1981.

Sizer, Theodore R. *Horace's School.* Boston: Houghton Mifflin Co., 1992.

Vygotsky, Lev. *Thought & Language.* Cambridge, MA: MIT Press, 1962.